Things I Can Do

 HOUGHTON MIFFLIN

Boston • Atlanta • Dallas • Geneva, Illinois • Palo Alto • Princeton

PETER SLOAN & SHERYL SLOAN

I can ride a bike.

I can catch a ball.

I can dig a hole.

I can mail a letter.

I can read
a book.

I can paint
a picture.

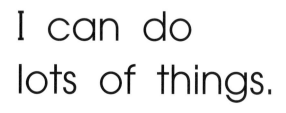

I can do
lots of things.